A Simple Walk
with
Jesus

My Personal Journey

Cynthia M. Ackerman

A Simple Walk with Jesus: My Personal Journey
Copyright 2018 by Cynthia M. Ackerman
Published by 5 Fold Media, LLC
www.5foldmedia.com

All rights reserved. No part of this book may be reproduced, stored in a retrieval system, or transmitted in any form or by any means-electronic, mechanical, photocopy, recording, or otherwise-without prior written permission of the copyright owner. Names have been changed to protect the identity of some people mentioned in the book. The views and opinions expressed from the writer are not necessarily those of 5 Fold Media, LLC.

Unless otherwise indicated, all Scripture quotations are from the New King James Version®. Copyright © 1982 by Thomas Nelson. Used by permission. All rights reserved.

Quotations marked (NIV) are from the HOLY BIBLE, NEW INTERNATIONAL VERSION®, NIV® Copyright © 1973, 1978, 1984, 2011 by Biblica, Inc.® Used by permission. All rights reserved worldwide.

Scripture quotations marked NLT are from the *Holy Bible,* New Living Translation, copyright © ©1996, 2004, 2007, 2013, 2015 by Tyndale House Foundation. Used by permission of Tyndale House Publishers Inc., Carol Stream, Illinois 60188. All rights reserved.

ISBN: 978-1-942056-70-6

Library of Congress Control Number: 2018936417

Printed in the USA.

Dedication

I dedicate this book to my Lord Jesus Christ, who saved me, changed me, and loves me unconditionally. I thank the Lord for inspiring me to write this story and for the courage to be transparent. I also thank the Lord for opening the doors for this project to be completed and sent out to touch others.

I thank my husband and my family for their support and for always believing in me. I thank all of the people who helped me edit and gave me encouragement with this project. I also thank the people who have kept this project and me lifted up in prayer.

Contents

Introduction	7
Chapter 1: Family Life	9
Chapter 2: Faith	13
Chapter 3: A Father's Love	17
Chapter 4: The Best and Worst of Times	23
Chapter 5: Second Chances	31
Chapter 6: The Love of God	41
Chapter 7: Fear	49
Chapter 8: Trusting God	53
Chapter 9: Another Spirit	59
Chapter 10: Time for Change	63
Chapter 11: Submission	69
Chapter 12: God's Timing	73
Chapter 13: Hearing from God	79
Chapter 14: The Glory of God	85
Chapter 15: Transformed	93

Introduction

I have seen many miracles in my life, and I believe that God showed me these to build up my faith. Now God has inspired me to share my story with others. This story will take you through my life, the good and the bad. You will see how God has been by my side through it all. He never gave up on me and even pursued me when I rejected Him. As a youth I let negative thoughts and oppression fill my life, but God has turned it all around for good.

When I turned thirty-nine years old, a car accident shook my very foundation. This was a turning point, and I started truly seeking God. I was no longer the same person I was before. The trials in my life have strengthened my faith, and I am learning to trust God in everything. The Lord has taken away my fear and given me a new foundation in Christ. Even on my toughest days, He was there protecting me and carrying me, even when I could not walk on my own. He has taken my low self-esteem away and replaced it with a trust in God that strengthens me. I started with a knowledge of Jesus Christ at a young age, but I now have a personal relationship with Jesus that has

A Simple Walk with Jesus

changed me deep within. I have experienced the power of God and His love that can never be duplicated. I long for the presence of God to be with me in all I do.

This story is told from my perspective, and hopefully by the end it's from God's perspective. I have had many tests and trials, but I have always turned to God and He has pulled me through. I hope that sharing my story will bring hope and life to a dying world. If you learn to trust God in all things, it's amazing what God will do. Once you know the love of God and His amazing grace, you will never be the same.

Chapter 1: Family Life

"And now abide faith, hope, love, these
three; but the greatest of these is love"
(1 Corinthians 13:13).

I grew up in a busy neighborhood near the city, but just far enough away that I felt like I was in the country. I was a city girl with a heart for the country. I had a large yard with a deep creek that curved through it. The backyard was split by the creek and had a bridge that connected the two yards. There was a big wooded area behind our property with a dirt road that was used for dirt bike riding. Our backyard was like a playground with a basketball court and a small building that could be used for many things. My yard was my refuge and gave me a sense of peace and a love for nature. My brothers and I would have parties in the back, and I would have my friends over to swim in our three-foot pool.

I remember sitting on the bridge with my friends, watching the water in the creek flow over the rocks; we would just talk and relax. The road we lived on was in a section with about five other roads that were separated from the city schools. Our bus ride to our school was a long way, but I believe it was worth it. There were many children who lived near me who were close to my age. My best friends lived across the street, and it was nice to always have someone to play with.

God blessed me with a very loving family, consisting of my parents and two brothers. My brothers and I are about eight years apart in age and I am the middle child. We didn't really get to know each other until we were older because of our age difference. My brothers mean the world to me.

My mother was a good role model for me growing up. She always saw the good in people and was always there to help when anyone needed her. Her love for God and her love for people was very evident. She worked as a waitress in her younger days. My mom had a servant's heart and always cared for people. Many people called her an angel. She grew up in the Catholic faith and attended Catholic school. Someone told her that she should become a nun, but when she met my dad, that was out of the question. It was love at first sight.

My father was unique in many ways. When he was young, he was a model, a chef, and eventually became a salesman and owned and operated his own business. He had a bold personality and people always knew when he walked into a room. He could be very sarcastic but in a fun and loving way. He liked to make people laugh and brought life to any situation. I loved listening to my father singing around the house. My parents laughed

Family Life

about how he had wanted to be a singer, but my mom had told him that he couldn't carry a tune. The memory of my father singing always brings me comfort. My dad liked flashy cars, big boats, and expensive jewelry, but he also had a big heart. He seemed to know everyone, and everybody knew him.

My dad and I had a special relationship. I was the only girl, so I felt like I was a princess. I was his baby girl, his sweetheart, and he wouldn't let me forget it. Every time I saw him, no matter what age I was, he expected me to greet him by giving him a kiss and saying, "I'm your baby girl and sweetheart." He was heartbroken if I forgot. I loved my father so much that I couldn't stand the thought of him being upset with me. He never had to spank me because all he had to do was raise his voice and my heart was broken. I would cry so hard it was hard to stop. Even after I was married, he still had that effect on me.

My mother and father were married when they were both seventeen years old. They were very young, but very much in love. He was Methodist and my mom was Catholic, so one of them had to change religions in order for them to be married. Things were very different back then. My dad wouldn't change, so my mom decided to switch to the Methodist faith. The Catholic church was very much against her switching religions, but this didn't change her decision. Their marriage through the years had many ups and downs, but their love for each other never changed.

A Simple Walk with Jesus

In my teens my dad was the owner and salesman of a siding business and my mom was the secretary and bookkeeper of his business. This kept my mom very busy and close to the phone at all hours of the day. The business eventually consisted of my whole family as my brothers both took salesmen positions. I was planning to step into the secretarial position when I graduated, but I decided to take another path. The stress in our family increased tremendously because of the business. You could feel the tension in the air when you walked through the door and it never went away. I'm sure the stress contributed to my father's early death at fifty-eight years old. My parents celebrated their fortieth anniversary before my father passed away in 1988.

Chapter 2: Faith

"Now faith is the substance of things
hoped for, the evidence of things not seen"
(Hebrews 11:1).

As a small child of seven, I remember coming home from school and realizing that my parents weren't home. As I walked from the bus to the house, my heart sank because there were no cars in the driveway. My mother was always there to greet me when I walked through the door. The door was unlocked so I could get inside, but the house felt dark and quiet, which frightened me. I looked down the hall, and there was Gigi wagging her tail. Gigi was a small gray poodle with really soft curls. She was always there for me, especially when I felt alone. I sat on the floor next to her and we snuggled.

As the minutes passed, I felt more worried and afraid. This was the first moment that I could remember fervently praying and knowing that God was really there. I asked the Lord to please keep my parents safe and bring them home to me soon. Petting Gigi helped take away some of

A Simple Walk with Jesus

my anxiety, but I was still getting more nervous by the second. After about five minutes, which seemed like an hour, my mother walked in the door. This was the first time I knew that God heard me and answered my prayer.

In the back of my mind I always had faith that God was always there. I know I learned about Jesus in Sunday school, but I had a deeper knowing that didn't come from there. I believe God has always been showing me Himself, even when I didn't understand. I always had a sense that He was listening. When I was a pre-teen I started writing in a diary, and that was my conversation with the Lord. I always began writing with "Dear God…." I knew He had heard me and helped me since I was very young.

When I was in sixth grade, I longed for new friends because of my low self-esteem. I felt like nobody liked me. I prayed every day for weeks, maybe months, that God would give me a new friend, even a boy who would like me. I was desperate! That coming school year, a new family moved in around the corner from my house. There was a sister and a brother who were both around my age. She became my friend and he became my boyfriend on and off for a while. He was very outgoing and his personality seemed bigger than life. I felt special because he liked me. My faith grew because God had answered my prayers in a big way by bringing these friends into my life. It might not seem like a big thing, but it was a miracle in my eyes and I knew that God had done this

14

Faith

miracle just for me. This girl and boy would never know how important their friendships were to me.

Through the years, I heard of amazing things that happened with my relatives, which increased my faith. I was told that one of my cousins regained the sight in one of his eyes that had been blinded from an accident. The doctors didn't expect him to ever see with that eye again. An uncle of mine had a major heart attack and was pronounced dead three times. The doctors were amazed that he kept coming back. They called him the Miracle Man. These miracles were starting to shape my life into trusting God. I believed God was in charge of it all. These miracles were showing me how good God is and how much He cared for us.

When I was a teen, God was drawing me closer by putting people in my life who might influence me to follow Jesus. I remember a girl who invited me and my friend to her church to see a movie. We watched the movie and then she wanted us to meet the minister. We went to his office and sat as he talked about Jesus. I remember the minister asking us a question that didn't make sense to me. Fear rose within me, and I just wanted to leave. I believe that he wanted us to accept Jesus into our hearts but I didn't understand. My fear put up a wall that kept God from getting any closer.

When I was a little older, maybe around seventeen, I went to the movies to see a rock opera about Jesus Christ; it was a musical about Jesus's life and crucifixion. It was a very controversial movie at the time with some churches

A Simple Walk with Jesus

because it told the story from Judas's point of view. I went to see it with my friends and it made a real impact in my life. Ted, the actor who portrayed Jesus, was a very gentle man with a large voice. He sang with so much power and emotion that it pierced my heart. I believe God used him in a mighty way to touch hearts for Jesus Christ. I know this movie awakened something deep inside of me.

As I watched, Jesus became real to me. God touched my heart as I saw how Jesus lived and loved people. He was so meek and mild but yet so strong and powerful. I already knew the stories about Jesus and believed He was the Son of God, but now He was becoming real to me. Now I saw Him as a real man *and* the Son of God for the first time. I saw how obedient He was to His Father in heaven and how He loved people more than Himself. I saw Him humbly accepting the course God laid out for His life. The crucifixion was the hardest part to watch.

After watching this movie, I couldn't sleep for a week. The songs kept repeating in my head and the tears kept flowing. My heart was crushed when I realized what we did to Him, the Son of God; I couldn't stop crying. I finally started to understand the price Jesus paid as He lay down His life for us. I couldn't get Jesus out of my mind for days. This was a turning point in my life when I really wanted to know Jesus and my love for Him grew.

Chapter 3: A Father's Love

"But you are a forgiving God, gracious and
compassionate, slow to anger and abounding
in love" (Nehemiah 9:17, NIV).

My parents were always very protective of me. They tried to shelter me from anything that they thought could harm me. When I was young, my friends were playing outside; my parents wouldn't let me cross the street alone. There was a younger girl who lived across the street who came over to walk with me across to the other side. It was very embarrassing for me because she was a couple years younger than me. I always got teased about this. Even at my wedding, her father brought it up and we were laughing about it. I can laugh at it now, but it was embarrassing then.

When I was eleven years old, my parents wouldn't let me ride my bike in the road. All of the kids in the neighborhood would be riding in the street and I had to stay in my driveway. One day I decided to do it anyway

A Simple Walk with Jesus

and I rode with my friends down to the corner. My older brother was driving by and stopped to yell at me. He said he was going to tell my parents so I rode back to my house and stayed there, but I don't think he told them about it because I didn't get in trouble.

When I was in middle school, my parents finally started to give me some independence. I met new friends and joined some clubs, but I still had low self-esteem. One day in seventh grade, I was invited over to a new friend's house to stay overnight. It was very surprising that my parents let me go because they didn't know this girl or her parents. If I only knew then what I know now. The minute I arrived at her house, I knew I wanted to go home. I didn't say anything for fear of what my friend would think of me. I was so uncomfortable, and I soon found out that my friend and her sister didn't have the same values I had. These girls were rude to their mother and wouldn't take "no" for an answer. Her sister and her friend hung out with us all weekend. The first thing we did was walk the streets, and they did some destructive things on the way. I wanted to go home, but I never said anything. When we finally went to sleep, I didn't sleep very well.

In the morning, they wanted to go to the beach or go shopping downtown. I didn't want to do any of it but I went along anyway. They decided to take the bus downtown to go shopping. I was nervous because this was the first time I'd even been on the city bus and I had never been downtown without my mom. I survived the

A Father's Love

bus ride and then we went shopping from store to store. We went to expensive stores and they tried on clothes while I stood and waited. I had no money and no desire to look at clothes. They must have bought some things because I remember holding their bags while they were looking for clothes.

Our last stop was at K-Mart and it turned out very eventful. While they were looking at clothes, a man came up to my friend and said something to her; then they both walked to the back of the store. I was afraid because I thought he was going to hurt her. I was so naïve that I had no idea that he was the security guard at the store. At that moment my knees felt like jelly and my heart was pounding while I stood and waited. As I looked up, I saw the same man come over to me and tell me to follow him too. So I did. My heart was racing and my legs trembling as I followed him. I still had no idea what was going on. We entered this small room where my friend was sitting. There were empty bags and new clothes sprawled on the table. The security guard asked me which of the clothes were mine. I couldn't believe they had stolen all these clothes. I burst into tears and said, "None of them!" I could hardly speak because I was crying so hard. I think I cried for an hour nonstop. He asked many questions and then called our parents. He couldn't get an answer at either of our houses. He told us that if he didn't get a hold of them, we would have to go to a juvenile detention home. This made me cry even harder. A while later, a policeman walked into the room and we had to follow him through the store to the police car that was parked

A Simple Walk with Jesus

out front. We both entered the backseat of the car and rode to the police station.

When we arrived, they took more information and then continued calling our parents again with no luck. Again they mentioned that we would be going to the detention center if they couldn't contact our parents. I was still sobbing. I had never cried so much in my life. Finally, we found my grandfather's phone number and they contacted him. He was the last person I wanted to know what had happened, but I was glad he found my mother. My mom and my older brother came to pick me up. I was incredibly relieved, but didn't want to leave my friend there alone. Even in all this chaos, I still cared about her. When my mom arrived I asked if we could wait for the police to contact my friend's mother and she yelled, "No!" I never saw my mom so angry before.

She took me home and I went straight to bed. My body was shaking with fear, thinking about what my father would do. I was sick to my stomach and wondering when he would be home. It seemed like hours later when my father finally arrived. He came into my room and sat on my bed to talk to me. I couldn't even look at him and my heart was pounding out of my chest. I don't even know what I was expecting because I had never been in trouble like this before. My fear multiplied and my imagination ran wild. He took me by surprise by being calm and quiet. His response was very different than my mother's had been. I found out that he had already gone and talked to the security officer; the officer was convinced that I

A Father's Love

hadn't shoplifted and that my parents should keep a close eye on me and keep me on the right track. The security guard must have known that I didn't participate in the shoplifting, so he got rid of any documents that had my name on it. I was greatly surprised to hear this; it was a great relief.

This was a point in my life when I began to open my eyes to the world around me and stop being so naïve. I started learning how to make better decisions and not just go along for the ride. I thank God for the opportunity to be freed from this horrible ordeal. I believe this was God's way of teaching me and protecting me at the same time. I could have had a completely different outcome if I didn't have such a loving father. He showed me unconditional love that day. Even though I was guilty by association, my father didn't punish me or put blame on me. He helped me and loved me through it. I believe the love he showed me was like that of our heavenly Father. I received a taste of God's love that day. I also learned a lot about life and myself that weekend.

Chapter 4: The Best and Worst of Times

"And those who know Your name will put
their trust in You; for You, Lord, have not
forsaken those who seek You" (Psalms 9:10).

When I was in tenth grade I made a major decision—I decided to take cosmetology. At first I was afraid that my father wouldn't let me, especially because I was taking business classes so I could eventually work for him. I was planning on being the secretary for my dad's business. I finally got the courage to ask my dad if I could and he said yes. I was so excited that I could live out my dream. Ever since I had been a young girl, I had wanted to be a beautician but I never thought that it could actually be a reality.

In elementary school, there was a cosmetology class nearby. On special days, someone from cosmetology would come over and ask my class if anyone wanted their hair done. (They practiced on us!) I loved going to get my hair done. I always got ringlets in my long

A Simple Walk with Jesus

dark hair. I felt like a princess when they were done with me. Sitting under the dryer watching all of them work was a mesmerizing experience. From that time on, hairdressing was deep inside of me, even though I didn't think anything would ever come of it. In ninth grade I attended a tour of the cosmetology classroom for the first time. That's when I knew I really wanted to do it. I started cosmetology in eleventh grade, and it was the best part of my day. I was very shy and afraid of working on people at first, but my teacher helped me come out of my shell. I slowly found the joy of what it was like to make someone happy by doing their hair. I knew that God put that passion inside me to bless people, which in return also blessed me.

The year I graduated was a very special one for me. I graduated on the honor roll and received my cosmetology certificate too. I also passed my state board exams and received my cosmetology license. I got a job right after school as a shampoo girl and then was promoted to hair stylist. I passed my driver's test and bought a brand new car. It was a very exciting year.

While in high school, my close friend introduced me to a boy named Rick who she knew from her camp out near the lake. I enjoyed meeting new people I didn't attend school with because I could be myself, free of preconceived ideas. I wasn't popular in school, and it was easier to be with people who didn't know how insecure I was. I was from the city and Rick was from the country, so we didn't seem to have much in

The Best and Worst of Times

common, but I knew he had a tender heart under all that roughness. We lived forty minutes apart so we only saw each other on weekends, but after a while our relationship became more serious. We dated four years before we got married. We had our ups and downs along the way, but he was my one and only true love. We had a beautiful wedding when we were both only twenty years old. We were young and immature, but we had a strength that would keep us together.

Two years after our wedding, God blessed us with a son, and then a daughter three years later. After our son was born, we decided to move near Rick's hometown near Oneida Lake. We took a risk and bought a handyman special. Rick is a carpenter and he comes from a family of carpenters, so we saw the possibilities. Our finances were limited so we took one step at a time with what we had. It wasn't easy raising a family in a house that needed so much work, but we survived. The house was in a good location—in the country with five acres of land, and it was a lovely area to raise children. I also found a new job at a hair salon nearby. The new salon was a down-to-earth, very comfortable place to work. It was a new beginning for Rick and me and our family.

With all of the busyness and changes in my life, I became distant from God. I knew in my heart He was still there, but I had new friends, family, and new challenges that drew me away. I became content with my life without God in it; but when our children

A Simple Walk with Jesus

started to grow, I had a need for them to know God as I had in my youth. It suddenly became very important for me to get involved with a church that would bring us closer to God. We had moved away from my church in the city, so we needed to find a church near our new home. I attended a few different churches around the area, but I didn't find one with which my whole family felt content. Finally, I checked out the Presbyterian church that Rick belonged to as a child. It was five minutes away from our house, and we all liked it very much. Our children attended Sunday school, junior choir, and handbell choir. I taught Sunday school for a few years. We were very active and glad to be there. The kids and I went to church every Sunday. Rick went on holidays or when the children did something special. He always had work to do around the house when he wasn't working on his job. I believed I was doing all the right things for my family.

Right before we moved from the city, my father was diagnosed with throat cancer. It was difficult to be so far away, but the decision had been made and we stuck by it. I did a lot of traveling to see my dad, especially when he was in the hospital. I thank God for the family and friends who took care of our son so it was possible for me to spend this time with him. My father wasn't diagnosed with cancer right away. For months he had a sore throat, which the doctor thought was an infection so he kept giving him antibiotics. It didn't help. He kept getting worse. When it affected his ability to swallow, he was finally sent to a specialist.

The Best and Worst of Times

They found that he had a large tumor on his larynx. It was terrible to think that it could've been detected earlier before it enlarged. He had a major operation to remove the cancer and also received radiation. He made it through the operation, but it was stressful and he was very depressed. The doctor removed his voice box to make sure the cancer was removed. They also removed lymph nodes and muscle in his neck and arms, which made him very weak. My dad was a salesman with a strong personality, and without his voice he felt inadequate. I had a hard time understanding why he wasn't happy to be alive. Every time I visited him, he teared up and cried. I was upset that he seemed to be giving up. I know now that I should have had more compassion and patience with him. I was so happy that he was alive that I didn't see the struggles he was enduring.

Five years later, my father went for his five-year checkup. The doctor told him good news—there was no cancer, but they found something else. They found a small aneurysm in his aorta. The doctor didn't seem very concerned because it was so small. There was a possibility that he could live with it for years with no problems. Maybe he wasn't a good candidate for surgery because of his previous surgery. He didn't handle this news well and was very upset. It took the life right out of him. During these five years my mom and my brothers had kept the business going with my dad's help. The whole family felt pressured already, but now the stress level rose even higher. One winter

A Simple Walk with Jesus

evening my dad went outside to clean snow off his vehicle, and he felt a pain in his arm that he knew was serious. They called 911, and when they arrived they thought he just pulled a muscle. It took my parents a while to convince the EMTs that this was more serious than that. They finally took him to the hospital and everything spiraled from there. My father was in the ICU for a week and failing fast. His mind was disoriented and his organs began shutting down. It was a terrible time for all of us. It was hard to watch someone I loved suffer so much. That night I prayed that God's will for him be done. It was a hard prayer to pray because I didn't know what God's will was, but I knew it would be best for my father. We received a phone call in the middle of the night telling us that he passed away. I believe in my heart that it was God's will for him to go that night. I knew that he was with Jesus and not suffering anymore, but I still cried for hours uncontrollably.

My family had a lot of healing to go through after that. The day my father passed away, I was in the process of buying equipment for my new salon that I was opening in my house. My father was very proud of me opening my own salon. He had always had big dreams for me. My grand opening was to be in a few days. I decided to keep that opening date because I knew my father would want me to do it. I knew in my heart that this was God's plan. I wasn't very busy at first so I had time to settle into my new business. This salon was a good fit for me. I could be home with my children

The Best and Worst of Times

and also contribute to our finances. It was also still a passion of mine to be able to touch people's lives by making them feel better about themselves, whether by doing their hair or through our conversation. I received a great deal of joy in my work. I have always been thankful that my family supported me in this new endeavor.

Chapter 5: Second Chances

"Yea, though I walk through the valley of
the shadow of death, I will fear no evil; for
You are with me, Your rod and Your staff,
they comfort me" (Psalms 23:4).

Through the years, my life became very busy. I started working in my salon at home part time and another salon part-time. I was active in our church, a 4-H leader, and also very involved with our local community club. Our children were in sports, 4-H, band, and choir. There were many games and concerts to attend, and I tried to make it to every event that they were involved in. Volunteering became like second nature to me. It was very fulfilling, but instead of making money it usually cost me money. With everything our kids did, I had no time for myself or my husband, for that matter.

I really thought that I was doing all of the right things for my family. I wanted to be a good mother and a good wife. I know now that I was doing a lot of things, but God was out of the equation. I was so busy rushing to get

A Simple Walk with Jesus

everything accomplished that I wasn't paying attention to what was really important. I found myself in situations in which God was trying to get my attention, but I didn't understand that, and I didn't listen. Maybe what happened next was the only way that the Lord could reach me.

For about a week, every time I drove into an intersection a strange feeling would come over me. My heart would drop and I would get shivers all over my body. I didn't know what was happening and tried to ignore it. After a while, it began to freak me out. After a couple weeks of that, something happened that changed the rest of my life. I would never be the same again.

It was a normal day. I was trying to accomplish laundry, get my children off to school, and get ready for work. I had worked late the night before and had a big day ahead of me. I was way behind on the laundry and had to clean my salon before I started work. I also had to bring my son to school because he had missed the bus. I was in a hurry, so I just put on a pair of pants and threw a jacket over my nightgown. I figured that nobody would see me and I'd take a shower after I got home. Little did I know what was going to happen next.

My son and I got in the van and I rushed to the school to get him there on time. On the way home, I looked at the sky, and it was a strange color and quite foggy. I hadn't noticed that when I had driven to the school. There was a lot of traffic and I had to turn left. The car in front of me went through the intersection, and then I started to turn left onto the other road. As soon as I started turning,

Second Chances

I saw a vehicle come out of nowhere. I never saw the car coming and I don't think he saw me. It all happened so fast that I didn't have time to react. Right after our vehicles collided, I saw my body flying through the air from the driver's seat over to the passenger seat. My feet and knees smashed against all of the wooden shelving in the dash of the van. I landed on the passenger seat with my legs pointed up and toward the center of the van. I don't know how the seat belt released, but I know I had been wearing it. What amazed me was that I never hit my head, especially on the windshield. It felt like God lifted me up in His arms and gently deposited me on the passenger's seat. I know deep down that God protected me that day.

After the collision, my van was still going in the opposite direction of where I had begun my turn. It looked like I had just parked my van on the side of the road. I was leaning backward in the seat and struggled to lift my head and straighten my body in the seat. I finally sat up and saw the other vehicle in the field. I saw a man in the driver's seat, unconscious. My heart dropped and I felt sick when I saw him. He had hit a tree or a pole before going into the field. There were a couple of people who stopped to help, but I couldn't see where they were. I was hoping that they would go to the other car and save that man. I think they called 911 and were waiting for the ambulance. I was getting very upset to see nobody over at the other vehicle, and I began praying fervently, hoping God was listening. I tried to move to the driver's seat but it was difficult to move.

A Simple Walk with Jesus

When I finally moved over, my van started steaming and making strange noises. I saw people directing traffic and using their cell phones. The man in the other vehicle was still unconscious, and still nobody went to help him. I found it strange that nobody came to me to ask if I was OK. Maybe they thought I had just parked there. I kept praying quietly for that man, for God to keep him alive. I couldn't stand the thought of him dying. I knew I wouldn't be able to live with myself if he did. I decided to get out of the van so I could go help him. I tried to open the door and it wouldn't open. I got it to open just a crack and I kept pushing on it so I could squeeze through the opening. My body really hurt, but I was determined. My right leg had no strength in it and it hurt terribly. I finally got out. I tried walking toward the other vehicle but I only got a few feet and my whole body collapsed to the ground. My body was trembling and I couldn't control it. I looked over at that man; he was still unconscious so I kept praying.

A friend of mine was driving by and stopped to help. She came over to comfort me while I was lying on the ground. I was still in shock and couldn't stop shaking. She covered me with a blanket and rubbed my head. Nobody else seemed to know that I was even there. I am so glad she came to help me so I wasn't alone. The police and the fire department finally arrived. Someone was finally trying to help that man. When I looked over at him, his whole body was shaking and my heart dropped. I just kept praying silently, "Please God, let him live!" Now the police were getting information and the ambulances

Second Chances

arrived. The EMT asked if I was OK, and my friend said yes. I had to interrupt and tell him that I couldn't walk. I could hardly get the words out of my mouth. I was still lying on the ground, shaking uncontrollably. I guess my friend thought I was upset and in shock, which I was, but I was also hurt. Then my cousin showed up and took my friend's place. She went to the hospital with me. It was nice not being alone. When they put me in the ambulance, my body kept shaking. I shook so hard I thought I would shake right off the cot. I heard that they were going to airlift the man, but they were still having trouble getting him out of his vehicle. I think they used the Jaws of Life to get him out.

When I arrived at the hospital in Syracuse about twenty-five miles from the accident, I was still shaking uncontrollably. As I was checked by the doctors, my cousin stayed by my side. It was comforting to know she was with me. The doctors were teasing me because I was wearing a red silky nightgown under my jacket, or maybe they were serious. They asked me if I was coming home from work. I just snickered and said no. Boy was I wrong about no one seeing that nightgown! I was very bruised on my left side—my arm and breast were black. I had many tests and X-rays. I thought I would shake right off of the X-ray table. The shaking didn't subside for at least two more hours. The X-ray showed that I had a fractured hip.

By this time I was wondering why I hadn't heard them bring that man in yet. I didn't know if he was still alive,

A Simple Walk with Jesus

and I was a nervous wreck. Everyone was praying for him. I was nervous but also excited when they finally did bring him in. At least he was still alive. But at this point, I still didn't know how badly he was hurt. Some of his family were at the hospital, but I don't think the doctors had shared much information yet. We could hear them talking, and they had no idea how he was yet. Still shaking from shock, I didn't like the feeling of not having control over my body. My husband and my mother were on their way, and some relatives offered to watch our children, which was a huge blessing. Later I found out why it took so long for them to bring that man to the hospital—he was taken to a closer hospital first where he died five times, and each time they brought him back to life. Then they had him stable enough to send him where I was where they could do more for him.

I believe with all my heart that God answered our prayers that day. I was admitted to the hospital for a few days and I had many visitors. I was surprised at all of the family and friends who came to see me. I hated the nights in the hospital. I felt alone and vulnerable. I also had too much time to think.

I found out that the name of the man in the other vehicle was Pat. When the doctor came in to check me, I asked him if he knew how Pat was. He was resistant about telling me anything but he did tell me that he was alive and they were running tests. Later when I was alone, I heard them call for his family on the loudspeaker. It scared me to death. I thought he might have died. Very

Second Chances

upset, I started praying harder than ever. The next time the doctor came in, I asked him again and he said that he was still alive. I was very relieved, but I knew he had a rough road ahead of him. The doctors would have to do a lot to make him whole again. That doctor kept my sanity by letting me know that Pat was still alive. I thank him so much for that. Wondering was torment.

The doctor told me I had a choice between having surgery or letting my hip heal by itself. I didn't want surgery if I didn't need it, so I told him that I would let it heal on its own. They said it would take six months. After a few days I was released from the hospital, and my mom and my husband took care of me and the kids. At first I had to stay in bed and keep my body straight. I could only sit one way and not bend or twist. Then I started using a wheelchair and finally crutches. Our living room was redesigned to be my bedroom for those six months. Rick made me a monkey bar over my bed so I could pull myself up and move myself in bed without hurting myself. He also made me a call bell so whenever I needed something, he would hear me and come and help me. He put a big old cowbell on a string and ran it through hook eyes, then through a cold air register from our bedroom upstairs down to my new bedroom in the living room. I could tug on the string from my bed and the bell rang upstairs. It worked very well and Rick was always there to help me. He took very good care of me. My mom worked hard cooking and cleaning.

37

A Simple Walk with Jesus

The accident happened right before Thanksgiving, so my mom had the holiday dinner at my house. Happily, the whole family came over for Thanksgiving. After my mom went back to her home, Rick had to take on all of the responsibilities of the house, our family, his job, and also take care of me. He taught our son to drive so he could get his license. Our church was very generous with lots of food and a donation for Christmas. Friends and family were wonderful and sent many cards, plants, and flowers. All of this was wonderful but all I could think about was how Pat was doing. I wanted so much to ask his family how he was and to say how sorry I was, but I was too afraid to talk to them. It is awful what fear can do to you.

When I went to my next doctor's appointment, I saw the same doctor who had given me information about Pat before. I asked him if he knew how Pat was doing. He said he was slowly improving. He had had a lot of surgeries but his spirit was up. At that time, he was in physical therapy. He had to learn everything all over again. I was very appreciative that this doctor told me all this, and I was excited that Pat was improving. Many people felt sorry for me, but I wasn't thinking about myself; all I could think of was Pat. I knew God was in control; after all, I could have been a lot worse. I knew God protected me.

Months later, I heard from a friend that Pat thought I didn't care what happened to him because I never attempted to find out how he was. I sent Pat a card to let him know

Second Chances

that I cared. Then one day I received something in the mail from Pat. It was coupons from his new business that he had just opened. He was a mechanic and he had opened his own garage. He wrote a note on the coupons that he wanted me to stop by sometime. He wanted to know how I was doing. What a shock it was to think that he cared about me! I wrote to him a couple more times and finally got the courage to visit him in person. I drove over to his new garage and introduced myself. I was very nervous to meet him but it helped that I knew that he wanted to meet me also. It took me a while to get the courage to walk through the door.

When I did I was amazed at his cheerful attitude. Once I talked with him and saw that he was whole and well, I knew this was a miracle. I was so excited to be able to talk with him and in awe of his wonderful attitude and his thankfulness to be alive. He had no bitterness in his heart and seemed excited to start anew. He told me that it was just an accident and that he believed everything happened for a reason. He told me how his life had changed dramatically and so had his priorities. He also said that God didn't let him remember all of the bad stuff. Pat still had health issues but he had defied all odds. The doctors hadn't expected him to ever walk or work again. God gave him a second chance, and He gave me one too.

Pat has been an inspiration to me because of his positive outlook and attitude toward life. Even after this horrific accident, he never gave up and fought the fight of his life. I learned a lot from how he handled this situation

A Simple Walk with Jesus

with so much grace. I thank God for how He turned this situation around and for the new life He gave Pat. I am blessed to know him. This accident was life changing. From this point on my life would never be the same.

Chapter 6: The Love of God

"The Lord your God in your midst, the
Mighty One, will save; He will rejoice over
you with gladness, He will quiet you with
His love, He will rejoice over you with
singing" (Zephaniah 3:17).

After the accident, I found that I was changing, but
nobody else was. I started seeing things in a new
way. My old music and television shows were not
important to me anymore. I began to recognize the negativity
that came upon me when I was listening to them. Rick and
I were so stressed out that we weren't communicating well
anymore. I had given little thought to the effect all this had
had on Rick. We argued all the time, and our kids got the
brunt of it. I didn't want to visit with our friends anymore
because I didn't want to be around any negativity. I knew
this upset him but I didn't know how to explain it to him.
Rick didn't understand my changes and neither did I.

Then, three nights in a row I had very vivid dreams that
really made an impact on me. It was the exact same dream

A Simple Walk with Jesus

every night, and I believe it was from God. The dreams were about the church I was currently attending. I had seen many events in which people were disrespectful toward God and had compromised the integrity of the church. I was troubled by what I saw and heard. The dreams showed exaggerations of the compromises I had discerned. They made it clear that it was time to look for a new church. I was getting stronger in my faith, and I could see the Lord confirming to me that it was time to move on.

I felt myself being drawn to a church that was more contemporary called Believers' Chapel Canastota. This was a big change for me and my family. Even though I knew my family might be uncomfortable there, I had a desire to go because I believed God wanted me there. One day I went to church with a troubled heart. Things were not going well at home. You could cut the tension with a knife. That day when the pastor started preaching, he taught about marriage and family. I was immediately overwhelmed. I felt like he saw right through me. I knew I was going to cry, so I quickly strode from the sanctuary and found my way to the back hall. The pastor's wife saw me and asked me if I was all right. I burst into tears and she prayed for me. I don't remember anyone ever praying for me like that before. I was filled with peace immediately. That's when I knew that this was the right church for us. I knew in my heart that God brought me there to help me and my family. I began to attend regularly and went to many classes. I had such a passion to know God more.

The Love of God

Believers' Chapel of Canastota was not a traditional church. Worship and prayer were emphasized, and I was learning the Word of God with an understanding that I never had before. They taught that the Holy Spirit lived within those who believe in Jesus Christ. I had never heard this preached before. They also taught that the Holy Spirit leads us, comforts us, teaches us, convicts us, and helps us follow God's plan for our lives. This was such an awesome revelation to me, and it changed my perspective and my life forever. The other churches had only touched on this subject.

In the year 2000, there was a guest speaker at church and he asked if anyone would like to accept Jesus into their heart or if anybody would like to rededicate their life to Jesus. I decided to rededicate my life to Jesus and then realized later that it was much more than that. I always thought I knew God, but now I was beginning to see that I wanted a personal relationship with Jesus. Within a couple of years, I was baptized in water and gave my life totally to Jesus Christ. This was a very exciting time. My heart was so passionate to know Him more.

Some churches say that when you get baptized in the Holy Spirit you will be able to speak in tongues, which is a heavenly language that you can't understand. I was nervous about it because I never heard of it before, so I fought it for a long time. Then one day when I was home alone praying, the Lord gave me some words that sounded like gibberish. I asked God to give me the interpretation of these words in English, so I would

43

A Simple Walk with Jesus

know what I was saying and could have peace about it. The Lord gave me the words right away: "I love You, Jesus!" This melted my heart because I realized I was praising God with these new words. That knowledge gave me peace to be able to speak in tongues and know that it really was a beautiful language between me and my Creator that only He understood.

Living in the country, we didn't have good television reception and we couldn't afford cable or satellite TV, but the Lord blessed us with a Christian television station. Since my accident, my faith had grown stronger by watching these Christian shows as they ministered to me. I know the Lord used every minute of my recovery to draw me closer to Him. One day while watching a show, I decided to join them in prayer. I kneeled on a pillow in front of the TV, bowed my head with my eyes closed, and began praying with all my heart. I don't remember what we were praying for, but I had an experience that I will never forget. I clearly heard the voice of God. It was a voice that I could hear and feel; it wasn't my own voice or thoughts. It was an internal, audible voice from God. He said to me loudly and clearly, "I love you." My immediate response was, "I love You too!" My heart swelled with passion and was beating rapidly. Filled to the brim with the love of God, I felt nervous and excited at the same time—nervous because the God of the universe just spoke to me, and excited because I had actually felt His love for me. Immediately I ran to Rick and told him, but I don't think he really understood. It was hard to explain, but it had been so awesome. My

The Love of God

passion to know the Lord just exploded. I was saturated with thoughts of God and nothing else mattered.

A major step in my spiritual journey was about a year later when our women's ministry held a retreat at a conference center in Cazenovia. I didn't have the finances to attend, so I didn't sign up right away. Finally, I was determined to go and I found enough money for the weekend. There were two guest speakers, Cheryl and Shannon, who would be praying and prophesying to the women who attended. I was a little skeptical. When it was my turn to be prayed for, I went to the front and sat down. This was all new to me and I didn't know what to expect. I had so much anticipation but was also very nervous. When they started praying for me, they were so accurate it was as if they knew me personally. I felt like somebody had just told them my whole life history, but I knew that wasn't possible. I was blown away by what they said.

Shannon prayed for me first and it was very encouraging. She even knew that it was difficult for me to attend and thanked God for bringing me there. It seemed as if Cheryl knew every little thing about me, including my struggles and feelings. It touched me deeply and I knew I was the only person who would truly understand it all, except for maybe my husband. Cheryl said that I kept hiding from God and that I was not going to hide from Him anymore. She talked about my low self-esteem and how God planned to impart confidence to me. She said I would see that I had great potential because of what God was putting in me. At the end of her prayer, Cheryl

A Simple Walk with Jesus

gave me a big hug and sang "Jesus Loves Me" to me. Once again, I felt God's love pour over me. I wept like a baby. This time of prayer touched my heart deeply and truly changed me forever. God kept showing me more of His love; it had been so amazing. When I returned home I couldn't wait to share this with my husband. I had received a cassette tape with the prayers and prophecy on it so I could listen to it again. I played the prophecies for Rick and he was shocked at their accuracy. Listening to it increased our faith in God and drew us closer to Him. This was truly a life-changing event.

Another special time in my life was when one of my favorite worship bands came to our church for two nights of special worship and ministry. I loved their music and their stories. It was an anointed time of worship and prayer. At one of the meetings a man from the band said that anyone who wanted to get closer to the Lord should come to the altar. He also said to come if you wanted to get rid of fear and hand it over to God. I wanted to get closer to the Lord so I went up to the altar and stood there. A member of the band walked over to me and began praying. He had shoulder-length brown hair and spoke very tenderly. He told me how God loved me and loved my smile. He told me that when I wasn't there, the Lord asked tenderly, "Where are you? Why aren't you here?" I began to cry! I wasn't expecting a prayer like that. I felt like Jesus Himself was talking to me. I didn't expect it to be so compassionate and intimate. I couldn't contain my tears. It hurt my heart to think that I had turned away from Jesus. Fear kept me away. The

The Love of God

man who was praying for me told me to get rid of my fear and give it to God, so I asked God to take it from me and I felt at peace. I felt Jesus' love for me that night.

Chapter 7: Fear

"I sought the Lord, and He heard me, and
delivered me from all my fears" (Psalms 34:4).

I started to see how much fear I had and how I needed to put my trust in God. My husband and I went camping in the Adirondacks one weekend. We had our tent set up and Rick was making a campfire. I could hear a storm coming from far away. I have always had a fear of thunder and lightning; it shook me to the core. The last place I wanted to be was in a tent surrounded by huge trees when that storm arrived. Rick had a different attitude about lightning. He loved to sit and watch it light up the sky. I think he saw it as God's light show. He had no fear whatsoever. I was nervous and didn't want to sit at the campfire, so I went into the tent and prayed. I could hear the thunder getting louder and closer. I was filled with fear; that storm was coming nearer. As I prayed and begged God to keep us safe, a sudden peace and calm flowed through me. My trembling stopped, and my fear was gone. I lay there in awe. When Rick came in, I showed him how calm I was; I wasn't trembling

A Simple Walk with Jesus

anymore. We were both amazed. A little while later, we saw the storm take a turn, and the thunder and lightning bypassed us. I knew God had answered my prayers. The Lord was teaching me to trust Him in the midst of a storm.

After attending Believers' Chapel of Canastota for a few years, the Lord put it on my heart to try out for the worship team. This was way out of character. I was shy and never wanted to talk in front of crowds. The thought of standing on a stage with everyone looking at me frightened me. Singing in a microphone frightened me even more, but I still had a desire to do this. I knew that the Lord wanted me up there, not because I could sing but because I love to worship the Lord. I believe He was doing a new thing by bringing the worshipers out of the congregation to lead people by example. The talents and instruments are good, but it's more about the heart. The Lord would rather have one person leading worship with a passionate heart than a big band with great musicians and many instruments whose hearts are not in the right place. What a joy it is to worship the Lord!

At this church an audition was necessary, and I had to fight my fear to go through with it. I could hardly get the song out of my lungs, and my voice was trembling. I prayed that if God wanted me on the worship team He would put me there, because in the natural I don't think I would have made it. I was relieved when the audition was over. I felt inadequate and embarrassed. I had to wait a couple weeks before I received an answer, and during

Fear

that time I just kept praying that the Lord would have His way. I finally got the answer that I made it on the worship team. I was excited and very nervous, but I knew that the Lord wanted me there.

My fear has also held me back from obeying God when I knew He wanted me to step out and approach someone and share His love. One day I was at a store. A man came in wearing old jeans and a T-shirt; his hair was long and gray, his face unshaven. He walked to the back of the store where the books were and was looking at the Bibles. From the moment he walked in, I knew that the Lord wanted me to talk with him. All of a sudden, I knew I should buy a Bible for this man and show him the love of God. I followed him to the cash register and heard him ask the cashier how much the Bible was. This gave me a little more time to get the courage to speak. When the cashier told him that it was a dollar, I wondered why he hadn't figured that out for himself. After all, everything in this particular store was a dollar. He walked back to the Bibles again, and I kept my distance in fear of him thinking I was a stalker. Then he grabbed a Bible and went up front and paid for it. I stood there watching, even though I knew what I was supposed to do. He walked out, and I walked after him. I thought that I could still go up to him, give him a dollar, and tell him that the Lord had wanted me to buy it for him. I noticed he was riding an old, beat-up bike. He got on it, and I slowly walked away, my body shaking. God wanted me to step out of my comfort zone, but I was too afraid. The man rode away on his bike, and I went to my car very discouraged. I

A Simple Walk with Jesus

knew my fear had held me back and I was mad at myself. I really think that God planted that man there to give me an opportunity to step out and do something for Him.

It took me a long time to stop beating myself up over this. I now see how the Lord used these experiences to help me grow into the person He made me to be. Every time I failed I learned a different lesson and grew from the situation. I found out that the Lord forgives me, but I have a hard time forgiving myself. He gave me so many chances to talk to that man, but I couldn't get through the fear. I am now learning to trust God more and step out without fear.

I am learning to get rid of my fear little by little. I have had fears operating in every part of my life, but I can feel God removing them slowly. I just need to trust Him and know that He will take care of me in any situation because He loves me. He is always with me and He will always bring me through. The more I learn of God's love, the more God transforms me.

Chapter 8: Trusting God

"Trust in the Lord with all your heart,
and lean not on your own understanding"
(Proverbs 3:5).

I have seen many healings done through people when they were receiving prayer. I've even prayed for someone and knew that God was doing something within them, either physically or emotionally. At times, I have felt great compassion for someone and knew the Holy Spirit was flowing through them to give them what they needed. It's very exciting to know that God can use us through prayer to heal people, break off bondages, and much more.

When I was forty-nine years old I had severe arthritis in my right hip (which is the same hip that I fractured in the car accident in 1998). Healing services became important to me because I needed my hip healed and I believed that God could heal it. I attended a few healing services at different churches and tried to have enough

A Simple Walk with Jesus

faith to believe that I was healed. I never got the healing that I was expecting. I went up front and announced my healing but my healing never stuck. It would begin hurting again as the night went on, and then I sometimes felt like I had lied to everyone about my healing. What a sorry state!

Then one day I went to a conference in Syracuse where an evangelist/revivalist was ministering. He traveled around the world and had a tremendous anointing from God on his life. The power of God was strong during that meeting. While he was preaching, Holy Spirit power came down in that place and touched everyone there. He said there was a healing anointing and that the Lord wanted to heal all who were there. I was excited because I had sought this healing for a long time. He started to speak out the healings that were manifesting. As he did, the person being healed needed to acknowledge that they had received their healing. He didn't lay hands on anybody or even come down from the stage. The power of God was so strong in that place that you couldn't deny that it was from God. My body started shaking as I stood there. I heard my right hip pop and my leg jerked; my legs were like jelly. I fell to the floor on my back. Thankfully, there were people around to catch us and let us down gently. When the power of God touches you, it can be hard to stay standing. I had no doubt that God was doing something in my body. Most of those there ended up on the floor. Then he said that someone had just been healed in their right leg. If you had been healed you were to stand up and walk. He didn't say the word

Trusting God

"hip," which put doubt in my mind, and I started having negative thoughts like, *What if I stand up and I'm not really healed? I would look stupid.* I was thinking about all of the other healing services that I attended and how I had never received healing; my doubt kept growing. I didn't want to be put on the spot and announce my healing in fear that it wasn't for me. But the man kept speaking out for that person to stand. He said it over and over again, but I was afraid and nobody else stood up. I believe that I was healed that night, but my fear and doubt took over. Upset with myself for my obvious lack of faith, I didn't talk about it to anyone.

That was my last try at healing services and I made an appointment with an orthopedic surgeon to see what needed to be done. The first doctor I saw was nice and funny, but I didn't feel confident with him at all. He actually tried to talk me out of it because he said I was too young. He recited every possible negative scenario in detail. I knew he wasn't the doctor for me. I knew I was younger than most people needing a hip replacement, but I had been in pain for so many years that I found it difficult to walk. I was too young not to get it done. I wanted to be able to live and enjoy life. I finally went and got a second opinion. This doctor was the complete opposite. He was very confident that it would be successful and a big improvement. He also shared all the things that could go wrong but was confident that the surgery would improve my quality of life. God also gave me signs that he was the right doctor for me. When I was on the phone with the insurance company, the lady told

A Simple Walk with Jesus

me that I had the best insurance, that the operation would be covered one hundred percent, and that my doctor was the best one out there. She reassured me that everything would go smoothly. I knew then that he was the doctor for me. When it came time to do the surgery, I knew God was in control.

The morning of the surgery I had no fear and was full of peace. While I waited, the doctors and nurses were scurrying back and forth getting everything ready. Before getting the anesthesia, the Lord put on my heart to call the doctor over. He was very compliant. I told him, "God is going to heal me using your hands!" He thought about it for a minute and said, "I receive that!" God is the ultimate Healer even when He uses people.

The operation went very smoothly and my recovery was quick. My husband took me to church only a week after I was home, and I was walking with a walker pretty well. I was filled with the peace of God and overcome with love. I was so excited that I could move around so well. During worship I lifted my hands up and sang to the Lord. I was so thankful that I could stand there by myself. God had healed me. Our pastor said that it was a miracle that I was there and doing so well. I was healing so quickly that only six weeks later, my husband and I went to Chittenango Falls and hiked to the bottom and back up to the top. It felt wonderful to be able to walk without pain and have strength in my legs again.

I learned something through all of this—God is our Healer and He will heal as He chooses. Sometimes it

Trusting God

will be through His power at a service; sometimes He will use people to work beside Him so He can work through them. I came to the conclusion that this had been a learning experience for me. I needed to get rid of doubt and increase my faith.

I also learned that God put us on this earth to help each other. He will also use people to bring His healing power to us as the Holy Spirit guides them and gives them wisdom. The Lord used this time of recovery to bring me closer to Him too. I had time to pray more, read more, and praise Him more. Sometimes you might think that God isn't there to help you, but He is always there, working things out behind the scenes. You don't always see what He is doing around you and for you. Sometimes God allows us to go through things to strengthen our faith. When we have nowhere else to turn, God is there. When we start trusting Him more with our situations, we learn to go to Him first and realize what we've been missing. Life is so much easier when God is first in our lives.

Chapter 9: Another Spirit

"For we do not wrestle against flesh and
blood, but against principalities, against
powers, against the rulers of the darkness
of this age, against spiritual hosts of
wickedness in the heavenly places"
(Ephesians 6:12).

In the year 2004, strange things started happening. I
would be awakened at 4:30 in the morning by noises.
It all started one night when I heard my phone ring,
but then realized that my phone was turned off. Then the
small stereo in my living room began coming on around
4:30 in the morning. This would happen maybe every
other day but not in a pattern. I started to think that God
wanted me to wake up so I could pray. So whenever I
woke up and the stereo was on, I would go downstairs
and pray. I found that this didn't happen when I had to
work the next day, which was good for me.

One night Rick woke up at 4:30 but the stereo wasn't
on. Then he realized that the kitchen clock had stopped

at 4:30. Things were getting stranger by the day. These things went on for months and I started getting very uneasy about it. I asked my pastor and some of my church friends for help, and received some much needed advice. I began to believe that God had nothing to do with it. I remembered how in the past my children often asked me if there were ghosts in our house because strange things happened sometimes. Cupboard doors opened on their own and lights came on in rooms that weren't occupied. I decided to get rid of the stereo. If it was God, He could wake me up another way. Then I would know if this was truly from God.

When I tried to unplug the stereo, I had a hard time getting my hand on the plug. The closer my hand got to it, the more it felt like there was a force field around the plug. I pushed through and finally unplugged it, and took the stereo out to throw it away. I suddenly felt uneasy and a little afraid about doing this because I knew there was something spiritual going on and it wasn't God.

After I put it outside, I went upstairs to my room to pray. I was praying intensely, but I still had fear of what was in my house. As I prayed, I saw a big gray cloud coming over me. It's hard to explain but even with my eyes closed I knew it was there. I rose up quickly and started yelling for it to leave my house in the name of Jesus Christ. I declared that I was a child of God and that Jesus Christ died for me and I belonged to Him. I told the Enemy that he had no place here! I quickly ran downstairs while commanding it to leave and opened the door and kicked it out. I knew

Another Spirit

I did the right thing because I felt the Holy Spirit envelop me with His peace. I was filled with peace and the fear was gone. I knew that God was protecting me and teaching me how to use the authority that the Lord had given me. What an awesome feeling to know that the name of Jesus and my faith had removed evil from my house. I thanked God for what He had done for me.

There were other times when I felt this force. I knew the Lord was teaching me that it wasn't from Him. I started to recognize the difference between the presence of God and the presence of evil. One day after the stereo incident, I was walking through a friend's house to get to the back door and found that I could not go any farther because I knew that something was there in the spirit; I could feel it. I felt that same force field and fear once again, so I didn't go any further. I just turned around.

Another time, my husband and I were checking out some property that was for sale. We were in the backyard and started to walk toward the woods when all of a sudden I had that feeling again. This was the first time that someone else was with me and I found out that only I felt this invisible shield in front of me. Maybe this force field was God's protection to keep me from going any further. I knew it was evil so I turned around and left. Rick kept walking around; it didn't seem to bother him, but I started praying. I don't have any explanation but I do know that it was not of God and I was sensitive to it. This was when I realized that I had some kind of discernment into the spiritual realm.

A Simple Walk with Jesus

One night I had a dream and I knew it was from God. In my dream I was hosting a baby shower in my home. There were people there I didn't know. Some of the gifts the mother received were very strange. There was a doll that seemed much too real and pictures of the baby that had real hair and really moved. Then I saw my friend walking around praying and I could tell she was upset at what was going on; then she left. I went outside and found another friend and was explaining what was going on. When I turned around to go back inside, there was something like a force field holding me back and I couldn't go any further. I was very upset because I couldn't tell the people inside what I was feeling and get them away from there. When I was writing down the dream, the Lord told me it was about divination. I didn't know what the word meant so I looked it up and found that it was a form of witchcraft, an imitation of God's creation. I believe the Lord gave me this dream to teach me about the spiritual forces that are out there and the ones of which I need to be aware. He was giving me the strength and boldness to speak against these things and speak the Word of God into these situations.

Since we removed the stereo and the spirit that was with it, we haven't had any things going bump in the night or turning on when they should be off. I know now how powerful my faith is and that I have the authority of Jesus Christ to speak to anything that is not of God and they will flee. I need to bring God's light into the darkness. The name of Jesus Christ is a powerful weapon for any believer.

Chapter 10: Time for Change

*"'For I know the plans I have for you,'
declares the Lord, 'plans to prosper you and
not to harm you, plans to give you hope and
a future'" (Jeremiah 29:11, NIV).*

At this time, I was having a hard time at my job working outside my home in a busy salon. There was so much bickering and gossip at work that it was very tense every day. I usually could stay out of it but somehow I kept getting in the middle instead. The hours were changing and I always seemed to have to work the hours that I didn't want. I believed God wanted me to look for something else, so I met with my pastor to make sure I was doing the right thing. He told me to pray and listen to what God wanted me to do. Through the months before having these thoughts, people kept asking me if I would go to their house and do their hair. I started to think that it might be an option. I could be my own boss, make my own hours, and spend time with people. That was one thing I missed while working in a busy

A Simple Walk with Jesus

salon. The company I worked for expected their stylists to be fast so more money came in. In my own salon, I had enjoyed taking my time and pampering people, and the conversation was always good. Now I could get back that personal touch I once had. Doing this made it possible for me to put God first on my agenda. I believed that if I put God first, He would take care of everything. My husband was behind my decision, whatever I decided. I kept praying and I knew what my answer should be. I decided to quit my job and put God first. I needed to get away from all the negativity and change my priorities. I knew it was all part of God's plan.

The same week I quit my job, I attended a prophecy class at church and a friend of mine told me that God wanted more time with me. I laughed and said that I was quitting my job so I could put Him first in my life. The same week I quit, my son moved to college. Then a few days later, my daughter talked about moving out of state to go to college. This was a shock to me and my husband. My daughter's friend had asked her to move in with her while she attended college in Virginia. Rick and I weren't prepared for her to move away and said no initially, but she wouldn't give up. I went to my room, sobbing, and prayed. Then I heard the Lord say, "Let her go." I knew then that it was God's plan, so we let her go. Everything happened all at once. When I saw my friend again, she laughed and said that God was clearly serious when He said He wanted to spend time with me. He had even sent the kids away so He could

Time for Change

have me all to Himself! It's amazing how God works in all the little details of our lives.

At first it was hard getting use to all the changes in my life. My business was just starting so I needed to build up my clientele. Business was slow at first but any money helped. My kids were gone and my husband was at work all day. I wasn't sure what to do with myself. When I wasn't working, I found myself sitting in front of the television. I couldn't stand watching some of the shows, but I felt drawn anyway. I would often get frustrated and not want to do anything. The next week was the beginning of a devotional life class at church; it was perfect timing. I was so excited because that was why I had quit my job—to spend more time with God and get to know Him more. When my class was over, my kids came back home from college and my business was doing well. I know that this was all in God's timing.

My business was doing well but it was not as busy as I would have liked. Not long after I started, gas prices skyrocketed. I had already established many clients for whom I had to drive twenty miles to get to their house. It was impossible to make money with the price of gas so high. I tried to add on a gas charge if they lived far away, but I didn't feel good about it. That's when I decided that I needed to look for another job. Soon after, something miraculous happened. One day as I was working, I saw one of my clients from the salon where I had worked previously. She asked me how I was doing. I told her that I might be looking for

A Simple Walk with Jesus

a new job. She told me that I could substitute teach in cosmetology where she worked. She thought it would be a nice job for me. I was intrigued. Cosmetology had been my favorite class in high school. I would be blessed to work there and be able to teach others my trade. I told her I would fill out an application and did so immediately. I had a nice conversation with the assistant principal; he urged me to also apply for a teaching assistant job for cosmetology because there would be an opening coming up soon. I felt very comfortable there and didn't hold back.

I never thought of myself as a teacher or a teacher's assistant but felt confident and excited by the thought of it. I knew I enjoyed being around teenagers because my daughter and her friends were always around and I enjoyed them a great deal. I had good thoughts about helping teens learn the trade about which I was so passionate. I remembered how I used to try to help other stylists with haircuts and the way they got upset with me. It was all making so much sense now. God had been getting me ready for this teaching position all along. My fears dissolved. I knew this was in God's plan because I had so much peace about it and everything was falling into place. I had to take a state test. I was worried about that a little because it had been so many years since I had gone to school.

I prayed before and during the test and God gave me clarity and helped me choose the right answers. I passed it with flying colors. Instead of being selected

Time for Change

for the substitute job, I was offered an interview for teaching assistant. I was shocked! There were many people being interviewed, so it was difficult. I wasn't sure how to answer their questions; I just tried to be myself. To my amazement, I was hired!

The first few weeks were not easy. Everything was new and everyone had to get used to each other. I needed to adjust to the teacher's expectations. I hadn't done many finger waves in the salon so I was a little bit rusty on them. I didn't know where any of the supplies were in the classroom, which made it difficult to help the students the way I wanted. Very few students made me feel welcome, and the rest of them tried to see how far they could push me. I did not give up and I kept pressing forward. My job got easier through the months, but it was always very challenging. Every year continues to get easier; it's fascinating to watch the cultural changes through the years. The groups of students are never the same but they all are a blessing to me.

I found that this campus had many Christians working there. There was even a prayer group that met once a week. I was excited to meet the people who were involved with the prayer group. It felt good to be able to share my faith with my coworkers. I knew that the Lord gave me this job to touch the lives of the students and maybe some adults, and I thanked Him every day for bringing me there. I felt that this was my ministry. While teaching these students a trade, I was also able

A Simple Walk with Jesus

to touch their hearts with the love of God and help them grow in character. God has put His love inside me for the students even through all the challenges. I will always be grateful for the Lord placing me in this position. What a blessing it is!

Chapter 11:
Submission

"Nevertheless let each one of you in
particular so love his own wife as himself,
and let the wife see that she respects her
husband" (Ephesians 5:33).

My husband and I met when we were both teenagers. We have been together for over forty years total—thirty-six married and four dating. When we exchanged our vows we both made a commitment that we would never get divorced. That mindset helped us get through many battles. We both changed a lot through the years, but we accepted those changes and began to grow with one another and not grow apart.

There was a season in our lives when communication was little to none between me and Rick. We didn't agree on many things especially about our children. My priorities became twisted because of the bitterness in my heart. I didn't even realize that the bitterness was there. All I could see were Rick's faults and not any of his good

A Simple Walk with Jesus

qualities. My thoughts were clouded and my heart was hardening.

When I wanted to get right with God, I read in His Word that I was to submit to my husband, so I asked the Lord to help me. My pastor began teaching me what submission really was. Submission wasn't something to which I would easily agree. I wanted my husband to change first. I thought that I could change him. I found out that God was the only One who could change my husband, so I started praying for him. Immediately God started revealing places in *my* heart that needed to be changed. The Lord was changing me and I didn't even know it!

Slowly, my heart began to soften. My attitudes changed, and I began to see the good in Rick again. The Lord was working on me and teaching me when to speak up and when to be silent. I noticed that things were changing in our lives. The more my heart softened, the more Rick changed. This took quite a long time, but God changed both of us. One day I brought a photo of Rick to my workplace and I put it on my desk. The next day when I walked to my desk, I immediately saw it and my heart flip-flopped in my chest. Butterflies filled me inside, and a rush of love poured over me. I was surprised at what I was feeling; I had so much love for my husband. It was amazing to feel that love strong once again.

Submission was a new word for me. Society has made women become the strong one in the family and sometimes the leader. God's plan was for the man

Submission

to be the head of the household and to love his wife unconditionally. The wife is to respect her husband and be a helper to him. She should love him enough to want to be there for him, even when it's hard. Neither the husband nor the wife is truly above the other because they should truly care for each other more than themselves.

Because my heart had changed, my perspective changed too. Now I saw a great many good things in Rick that I hadn't seen before. He cared for me; it was noticeable in the many little things he did for me. He wasn't obligated to do those things; he did them because he cared about me and wanted to make things easier and safer for me. He is a loving man, and I am grateful to God that He helped me see my own faults so He could change me and bring my husband and I back together.

Just because our hearts have changed doesn't mean all of our faults are taken away. My husband and I both still have many faults, but our love for each other is stronger than they are. Proverbs says, "Hatred stirs up strife, but love covers all sins" (Proverbs 10:12). This Scripture is revealed in my life. The more we love, the more forgiveness and understanding we have for each other. Through this process, our faith has increased and our love has endured. "A threefold cord is not quickly broken" (Ecclesiastes 4:12). The threefold cord represents Rick, me, and Jesus; Jesus is the strongest cord in our threefold cord. Because the Lord is entwined in our marriage, our marriage can withstand anything.

A Simple Walk with Jesus

That third cord strengthens our marriage, and as long as we look to God for help and don't take matters into our own hands God will bring us through.

Chapter 12: God's Timing

"The Lord is good to those who wait for Him, to the soul who seeks Him. It is good that one should hope and wait quietly for the salvation of the Lord" (Lamentations 3:25-26).

Sometimes we might ask God for something and we don't get the response that we were hoping to get. That request might not be part of God's plan or it might not be in God's timing. We live in a microwave society in which we expect things to happen immediately. We need to be patient and wait on the Lord. If I trust Him then I am not filled with anxiety while waiting. I am still learning this day by day. It is not an easy task. When you believe that God is for you and not against you, you can believe that whatever He does is what is best for you. The Lord is working in your situation even when you don't see what He is doing. He is never too early and never too late. He is always right on time. Sometimes we bring delays on ourselves. He might not give us what we want right away because He knows that we aren't

A Simple Walk with Jesus

mature enough to handle the responsibility. We might not be ready for the blessing and all of the abundance that accompanies it.

We can also hinder the Holy Spirit from moving; then the Lord will wait on us. Our hearts might not be set on God, but we expect Him to help us anyway. He might hold back until we realize we need to seek Him first. Believers' Chapel Canastota has participated in many parades through the years. The worship team usually has a float by which they bring music through the streets and praise the Lord. One year they were starting to line up in the parade, and it wasn't going quite as planned. It seemed as though nobody on the team was focused on God; they were being silly and some were not happy with the way things were going. There were big speakers so everyone would be able to hear them, but then the generator failed and those speakers were useless. That meant there was no sound and nobody was going to hear the voices and the instruments the way they should. It was very tense, and we weren't sure what to do. All of a sudden the Holy Spirit brought a song to our minds. One by one we slowly worshiped the Lord together. The song wasn't on our list and it wasn't rehearsed. We didn't have the music or the words, but everyone came together and worshiped the Lord.

From that point on, we were focused on God and the Holy Spirit took over. The generator started working and another generator came so we had more than enough. Our voices blended together and the sound was beautiful.

God's Timing

We were all in unity. All the bad attitudes were gone and we were about our Father's business. I was told that the two church bands (ours was one of them) sounded great, much better than the radio station. The Lord was glorified! Even in our bad attitudes and silliness, the Lord had His plans go through perfectly without a hitch when we focused on Him and not on ourselves.

Sometimes the Lord speaks to me through songs. I was alone listening to a song one day; as I began to sing, the words came alive. My spirit stirred up and my voice got louder and bolder. Something inside was bubbling up, and I knew I had to share this with the church. While I was singing this song, the Scripture from Ezekiel 37 about the dry bones came to me. I had a prophetic picture of God breathing His breath into our lungs, making us alive in Him as His mighty army. I felt Him telling me that we should praise Him with the breath that He has given us. Every time I heard this song, the Spirit of God within me confirmed God's message again. I believe this song was for the discouraged and downcast within the church. God is bringing life to His people. I tried to have this song sung during worship at my church but to no avail.

One day I was asked to do a devotion at our women's retreat. I was excited because I could finally share this song and what the Lord shared with me. It was then that I realized that it was all in God's timing. It had taken a few months to get the message out, but in God's perfect timing it was shared with the women of the church. I

A Simple Walk with Jesus

thank God for the patience and determination He gave me, which helped it come to pass. Since the women's retreat, that particular song has been released in our church and sung many times, and the theme has spread. I believe this made an impact in the kingdom of God. God is preparing us to be His mighty army!

The Lord has also touched me with songs that He has given me, psalms to write, and even melodies to go with a couple of them. One night during an intercessory prayer meeting, we were asked to write a psalm to the Lord. The words flowed from my pen, and when I went home that night the Lord put those words to a melody. The melody was in my head and I simply began to sing my psalm. I have written more than a dozen psalms since then and have a melody for another one. I thought I would easily find someone to help me write the music for the psalm because I didn't know how to read music and couldn't finish it by myself, but it just didn't happen. Feeling discouraged, I put it on the back burner and waited.

But that first psalm felt like it was straight from the heart of God. My heart still bursts every time I sing it. I had had such a passion to get it written so we could sing it, but every time I asked someone to help me, they said they would, but it never came to pass. There were times when I wanted to give it up, but then the Lord would put it on my heart again. It was on my heart for nine years. One day during worship the Lord told me to ask Brent to help me with my song. Brent was leading worship that day, and he is also a music teacher, so it made sense

God's Timing

to me that he would have the knowledge to be able to complete this task. But would he want to use his time doing this for me? I didn't know what his answer would be, but I knew I had to be obedient to the Lord and ask him. I was surprised at his response. He said yes and immediately started to work on it with me. Brent was very interested and helpful. He didn't waste any time. Within a few weeks he had the song completed. I was thrilled to see what he had done. After the song was written, I wondered if we would ever sing it in church. I'm usually on the worship team with Brent about once a month, so I waited until it came around to find out.

The day finally came when I was on the worship team with Brent, but something came up and I couldn't make it to church that Sunday. Brent sounded disappointed because we were going to sing my song. Finally, a few weeks later I was on the worship team with Brent again. I had waited for nine years for this day to come when we could worship the Lord with the song that He gave me. Even though I was nervous singing it, it felt wonderful to finally be able to sing it with everyone. I know the Lord was pleased.

The day that we sang this song happened to be the same day we had a guest speaker named Bill Yount at our church. I was excited to have him there because I'd read some of the prophetic words he had given the body of Christ; they were very encouraging. He was visiting for the weekend and ministered at our church and another church also. His teaching and prophetic words were just

A Simple Walk with Jesus

what we needed. It was as though he knew everything about us, and he encouraged and exhorted us. Bill is a very humble man and enjoyable to hear. I was blessed that we were going to sing the song I had written while he was there, not knowing what an impact it would make. Later I found out that Bill had asked the pastor if he could have a copy of it and they had given him one. I texted Bill and told him how blessed I was that he wanted the song. He told me that the song was just for him. That amazed me. Once again, everything is in God's timing. The Lord had everything completed in His time, not too early or too late, right on time. He wanted Bill to hear that song so he could be blessed by it, which blessed me and in turn blessed the Lord.

The Lord is taking me through a process. He has given me psalms to write. He has given me melodies and a passion to sing. He has given me someone who has that same passion and can help me where I need it. He has taken my fear away and given me more boldness to be able to sing. He has also surrounded me with people to encourage me. This is just the beginning. Who knows what God will do next!

Chapter 13: Hearing from God

*"And after the earthquake a fire, but the
Lord was not in the fire; and after the fire a
still small voice" (1 Kings 19:12).*

There are many different avenues in which God can speak to us. You can hear His still small voice if you listen with your heart. He might use other people to bring His word, or we may hear Him through reading Scripture as it comes alive. He can use dreams and visions to speak; He can also give revelation about a circumstance. When I'm writing, it seems like the Lord gives me the words to write. I seem to be able to hear Him more clearly when I write. It must be the way He made me. When I listen for God's still small voice and let the Holy Spirit lead me, every day is an adventure.

I have always written in diaries or journals to talk to God and share my heart with Him. When I got serious about following Jesus, the Lord often spoke to me while I wrote.

A Simple Walk with Jesus

I began to understand how much I was loved and how precious I was to Him. I believe the Lord was building me up to know who I was in Him. God was trying to break off my low self-esteem. Slowly I was beginning to see how precious I was in His eyes. He feels the same about all of His children, if only we would listen.

In 2004 I attended a youth conference with others from our church. Youth from many different churches attended the conference. I was one of the many chaperones. We stayed at a church in Albany and had an amazing time. Sleeping on the floor in sleeping bags, we woke to worship in the morning and continued in worship and prayer in the evening. We were blessed with worship, prayer, and the Word of God every day. They showed us how to evangelize in the city. I enjoyed every minute of our time there and left a changed person. This event was for the youth, but I had never experienced anything like it before, and it touched me deeply. The prayer was so intense that it brought many tears of joy and of sorrow. I felt incredibly free at the end of our time there, as the presence of God was deep and strong.

When it was time to leave and drive home, I could hardly concentrate on my driving. My mind was filled with praises to God. I tried to repeat what I was hearing, but the words wouldn't come out. They were fast and full of passion. I felt overwhelmed with God's love, and I believe I was hearing the angels praising God. It was an awesome experience but it made it hard to drive,

Hearing from God

as I could hardly concentrate on anything but God. Thankfully, the Lord made sure we arrived home safely.

When I got home, I felt great love and joy for everyone I saw. It became frustrating because the people around me didn't share in this awesome state I was in. After a few days, I was back to normal; it was like coming down from being high on life. If only I could have stayed enveloped in His love. The Lord did something inside of my heart and my soul during this conference that changed my thinking and healed my heart. It was just the beginning of what He wanted to do inside me.

The Holy Spirit and His still small voice has nudged me to do many things through the years. There was a day when the Holy Spirit nudged me to buy some yellow carnations to give away to people so I could put some sunshine in their day. I bought a bunch of yellow carnations at the florist to give them away. I didn't know who I was going to give them to at first, so I began at my church and gave a couple of them away. Then I wondered where God would bring me next. I drove toward Syracuse and made a few more stops on the way. It was fun to surprise people and bless them. I wasn't always sure what road to take to get to people's houses, but the Holy Spirit directed me and I never got lost once. I had so much fun that day. I received much more joy than the people receiving the flowers; the love from the people filled my heart to the brim. It was just a small act, but it was powerful because God was directing me. To follow the leading of the Holy Spirit was exciting. Every day became an adventure.

A Simple Walk with Jesus

The closer I got to God, the more passionate I was to know Him more. His presence became real to me, and I longed for more of Him. When I was at a women's conference, the speaker told me that when I was down God held me close to His heart so I could hear His heartbeat. That word stuck with me all year until I found this beautiful prophetic painting that touched my heart. I purchased it. It's a picture of Jesus holding His bride with her ear close to His chest and her hand on His heart, so she can hear and feel His heartbeat. Every time I looked at this picture, my heart swelled with passion. Then one day a Christian ballet company visited our church and performed for us. The leader of the company said, "God wants to hold us close to His chest so we can hear His heartbeat." When I heard this, I jumped out of my skin with excitement, and I told her about my picture. Later that day I was listening to a CD of a preacher; he was saying that God wanted to hold us close to His heart so we could hear His heartbeat. I couldn't believe that I heard that same thing again. God kept confirming this to me over and over again. My heart was full of love for the Lord.

God uses dreams and visions to speak to me also. One time during worship on a Sunday morning, we were singing and I had a vision of Jesus standing next to me and we were standing on a rock. All around us was quicksand, and people were sinking everywhere. Jesus reached His hand along with mine toward the people in distress. My arm and Jesus' arm were united, and we were pulling people up one by one out of the sinking sand, putting them on the solid rock. The vision wasn't long, but it

Hearing from God

made a huge impact on me. The song was over and we went to a new one but I couldn't stop thinking about the vision. It was amazing!

Sometimes God has granted me insight through dreams too. I woke from a dream one morning and immediately wrote it down. I got my Bible out and started looking for Scriptures and studying what the Lord had spoken to me. I knew this dream wasn't for me alone. I needed to share it with the church. God was sharing that we should be ready for anything the Devil threw at us; He wanted to strengthen and prepare us for the spiritual fight ahead of us. This is just one dream out of many that the Lord has given me.

Another way God speaks to me is by showing me something in the natural and then giving me a revelation in the spirit of what He wants to tell me. One day as I was looking in at a house, I noticed all the cracks in the foundation that I had never seen before. These cracks made me concerned about the strength of the foundation of that house. Then the Lord spoke to my heart that He wanted us to examine ourselves and find any cracks in our spiritual foundation. We needed to fill those cracks with the Word of God and seal them so the Enemy would not have any access. These cracks spread through any anger, bitterness, unforgiveness, greed, or the like that was present in our hearts. We needed to examine ourselves, repent, and let God's love seal up the cracks and make a sturdy foundation that would withstand any attempts of the Enemy to weaken us. We needed a strong

A Simple Walk with Jesus

foundation in the Word of God, not only in our heads but also in our hearts, so nothing could bring us down.

What an awesome thing it is to be able to hear the Lord in so many different ways. It brings joy to my heart to hear Him and obey and feel His love flowing through me. Sometimes I feel very confident of what God is saying to me—I know that I know that I know. I have no doubts inside me, and that brings power to my words when I speak the Word of the Lord. What a great work God has done!

Chapter 14: The Glory of God

"They shall see the glory of the Lord, the excellency of our God" (Isaiah 35:2b).

I believe that babies are sent from heaven and reflect the glory of God. The Lord has shown me His glory when I look at my grandchildren. When my first grandchild was in her mother's womb, I had an amazing experience. I went to see my daughter's sonogram and was blessed to be able to see my grandchild before she was born. It was exciting to see this tiny baby moving around inside her. As I watched the screen, the baby turned her head and her eyes met mine. We had an immediate connection like I have never had before and my spirit leaped inside me. We had a special connection and bonded; we would be close together forever. I felt like I knew her inside and out, even though she wasn't born yet. God knows us even before we are born. "Before I formed you in the womb I knew you" (Jeremiah 1:5). After she was born, when I held her she would look up and smile as she looked around at the ceiling. I always

A Simple Walk with Jesus

believed that she was looking at angels. Her smile was contagious and filled my heart with joy. Watching her grow and continue to seek God touches my heart immensely.

Almost seven years later, my next grandchild was born. I was hoping to have the same experience at her sonogram, but no. The technicians could never get a good visual of the baby, which was disappointing. It was frustrating that they couldn't get a good picture of the baby as they tried over and over again. I was fighting any doubt that came to my mind about the baby's health, and I never shared my thoughts with anyone.

The day she was born was a hard day. When she was born, she was quickly whisked away by the doctors and nurses. My daughter saw her quickly but wasn't allowed to hold her. Everyone was heartbroken and in shock. We had no prior knowledge of any health problems with the baby. She had a defective heart and many other issues. Still God showed His glory. With all of her defects, God made her heart so special that even though it shouldn't have been able to function, she lived. She has gone through two heart surgeries and will have more, but God has shown us His power and mercy through our precious little sweetheart. The Lord has tested my faith, and I sense that the test is now over. I thank the Lord for that. The Lord has her in the palm of His hand, and I need not worry because He is in control. She is a special little girl. She brings people together in prayer, which glorifies our Lord. She is another miracle

The Glory of God

the Lord has put into my life. I believe the Lord has big plans for both of my grandchildren.

> "'For I know the plans I have for you,'
> declares the Lord, 'plans to prosper you and
> not to harm you, plans to give you hope and
> a future'" (Jeremiah 29:11, NIV).

My favorite thing to do is to worship the Lord. When I am singing to the Lord, my heart is full and I feel His love. God's presence is like nothing I have ever experienced. It can be soft and sweet and it can be electrifying. Either way it is powerful and makes me long for more of His presence. Worship and prayer to the Lord are a huge part of my life now; I would have it no other way. God has touched me in many ways. He has taught me how to hear Him through reading the Bible, prayer, listening to other people, and even through hearing His still small voice, and sometimes His voice is a little louder. I have learned how to see God move and do things all around me. I have felt His touch when I'm in His presence, and it is overwhelming. I have even smelled the fragrance of the Lord.

During a worship service while we were singing with all our hearts, I smelled a sweet fragrance that kept getting stronger. I had never sensed anything so beautiful before. I asked other people if they could smell it and nobody did. Finally, I knew that it was a special fragrance from the Lord. I couldn't even describe it; it was beautiful and intoxicating. God has touched all of my five senses—the sense of touch, hearing, sight, smell, and even taste.

A Simple Walk with Jesus

"Oh, taste and see that the Lord is good;
blessed is the man who trusts in Him!"
(Psalms 34:8).

Yes, the Lord is good!

I also see the glory of the Lord when I am outside; God uses the trees, lakes, mountains, animals, birds, and all of the natural world to teach me things and bless me. I feel especially close to God when I am in God's creation. There is such a peace and rest when I am there among the trees, mountains, and lakes. God's beauty is glorious.

I attended a youth conference in Watkins Glen, New York with my daughter when she was a teen. Excited to go, I had never been there before and had only heard about the area. The wonder and beauty of the gorge and waterfalls were said to be spectacular. Much to my surprise, it didn't look like I thought it would. We weren't in Watkins Glen State Park and all I saw were buildings. There were teens there from all over the state with their chaperones. They had many activities, and at night we slept in the bunkhouses around the main building. Going from a small town to meet teens from all over the state was hard because we were all so different. Leaders from other areas let their groups say and do things that we wouldn't ever let ours do. Morality was somewhat lost in some cases.

I made friends with another leader who thought the same as I did. Both of us were rather frustrated. We were stuck with all of these people who were either obnoxious with a low moral barometer or they went to the other extreme

The Glory of God

and were legalistic. I just had a longing to see the gorge in the middle of all this. I felt the Lord nudging me to step away from all the clatter and go outside to seek Him. I finally got a minute away from all of the hustle and bustle. I took a walk outside and noticed an opening in the trees through which I could explore. I followed a trail until I found a large creek. The walls of the creek were high, full of shale and limestone. The water was clear and flowed over the shale, glistening in the sunlight. The rocks were fluorescent green; it was the most beautiful sight. I was mesmerized. God drew me to that particular area just to bless me. After soaking it all in, I went back to the chaos. I couldn't wait till the end of the meeting so I could bring the girls to this wonderful spot I had found. When it was over, we took a hike to the creek; it was so peaceful. It was much needed after the busy, noisy weekend. What a wonderful way to end our trip. God met us there.

One time my husband and I went to Chittenango Falls to take a hike. I was well into my recovery after having my hip replacement surgery. I was feeling strong and thought that the hike down the falls and back up would be good exercise. It felt wonderful to be able to use my hip again and be strong enough to hike. When we got to the bottom, we stood on the bridge and admired the falls. While I was watching the water flow down over the rocks, I noticed how it flowed through every little crevice and didn't miss a single crack. The rocks were saturated and washed clean. The water was so powerful I could feel its presence, even though it didn't touch me.

A Simple Walk with Jesus

Suddenly I could feel the Holy Spirit washing over me and cleansing me, just like the water from the falls. I received revelation that the Lord wanted to cleanse the church. His Holy Spirit wanted to wash over us into every nook and cranny of our hearts and souls, just as I had witnessed at the falls. I was able to share this with my church, and I believe it's a work in progress. This was an amazing experience with God.

On one of our trips to the Adirondacks, my husband and I vacationed in Old Forge and we stayed at a bed and breakfast on the Moose River. It was nice to be so close to the river because we had our own canoe with us. We took a relaxing trip down the river in our canoe and were hoping to come across a blue heron as we paddled along. I love blue herons because they remind me of a prehistoric bird.

As we glided across the water, this pretty little bird was flying near us and it seemed as if it wanted us to follow him. It would fly to one side of the river and stop at a tree and then fly to the other side farther down and stop. We were keeping our eyes on it while we were paddling. It kept going back and forth down the river, and we always seemed to be on its tail. Quite a ways down the river the bird took a turn, but it was still in our sight. It turned into a marshy area and flew into a tree. As we turned, to our amazement, there stood a large blue heron; the little bird was in the tree right above him. That little bird was directing us to this special place to see what we were hoping for. It was an awesome sight and such a blessing.

The Glory of God

We knew this wasn't a coincidence; it was a God thing. This is just one of the many blessings the Lord has given us. There are no coincidences. I keep my eyes and ears open to notice what God is doing all around me. Whenever we go to the Adirondacks, we see God.

A few years ago while camping, I was all alone at our campsite standing in the dirt; I looked up at the trees when I noticed how big they were. The wind was blowing and became stronger as I stood there. The tops of the trees were bending over in the wind from one side to the other. I felt frightened. Would the trees snap? But I still kept standing there as if I couldn't move. I felt the wind push me back and forth just like the trees, but then it seemed to shift. It began going in a circle like a whirlwind. I heard a whistling through the trees; God was singing over me. As I looked up, the wind swirled around me and it felt like I could have been taken up with it, but I stepped back and went inside our camper. It really felt like a big hug from God. The Lord was right there and I was having a close encounter with Him. I will always wonder what would have happened if I stayed there and hadn't stepped back. I love when God meets me wherever I am.

My husband and I love to gaze at the stars at night. It seems as though God always blesses me with letting me see the shooting stars before my husband does. When I look into the sky and think about how God put every star in its place, I am in awe. "When I consider Your heavens, the work of Your fingers, the moon and the stars, which You have ordained" (Ps. 8:3). One cool night Rick and

A Simple Walk with Jesus

I were standing around a campfire in our backyard just about midnight. We were having a great conversation about God and what He had done for us. All of a sudden we looked at the sky and it looked like it was dancing. There were different colors flowing through the heavens in waves, back and forth. The northern lights took over the sky and it was glorious. It felt like God was dancing over us. We did not know the northern lights would be out that night. Having it happen when we were just talking about how awesome God was made me believe that God was pleased with us. He had given us a glimpse of His glory.

We can experience God in many ways. These experiences that I have shared are just a few of the awesome ways that God has shown Himself to me. I am in awe of His beautiful creation and His amazing power. Nature is God's masterpiece for us to enjoy. The glory of God is magnificent.

> "O Lord, our Lord, your majestic name fills
> the earth!" (Psalms 8:9, NLT).

Chapter 15: Transformed

"But we all, with unveiled face, beholding
as in a mirror the glory of the Lord, are
being transformed into the same image
from glory to glory, just as by the Spirit of
the Lord" (2 Corinthians 3:18).

I will always have hope with the Lord in my life. No matter what I go through, I am always confident that the Lord is right there to help me. He has never left me even when I turned away from Him. When I decided to turn back to God, He accepted me with open arms. His love is pure and unconditional; He is a forgiving God. All we need to do is ask Him to forgive us and He is right there waiting, ready to forgive.

It's amazing even now how much He is changing me. My faith in God has increased and my fear has decreased. I am being transformed from the inside out. I am not yet where I want to be, but I'm not where I used to be (which is a good thing). The Lord isn't finished with me yet. There is much more to come! He has given me so

A Simple Walk with Jesus

much, and I need to share it with others. It has taken many years for the Lord to help me grow spiritually, but it's all in God's timing. I am learning more all the time. God always has something new coming just around the corner. God has proven to me over and over again how faithful He is. He has provided for us financially when we thought we could never make it. He has protected us in many ways. He has comforted me and given me peace, even in desperate times. He has healed and delivered me from my fears. God has transformed me from timid and fearful to the strong, fearless, and confident woman He sees through His eyes. The Lord has transformed my mind, my heart, and my character.

> "But the fruit of the Spirit is love, joy, peace, longsuffering, kindness, goodness, faithfulness, gentleness, self-control" (Galatians 5:22-23a).

I feel that the Lord has imparted these qualities into my spirit, and I long for them to flow out of me to others. I have learned to wait on the Lord and have more patience to see things come to pass than I used to have. I don't always get my way; I might have to wait until God changes circumstances or softens hearts, but I know that God is faithful and He will do what is best for me.

We all are children of God and He longs to have a relationship with us. I am blessed that I learned this and let Jesus in my heart before it was too late. We don't know what each day will bring, and it saddens me to see people without the hope of eternal life. What Jesus did for us on the cross is undeniably the greatest sacrifice that was ever made. Jesus is man and the Son of God. He died on the cross as a man but lives as the Son of God through the resurrection to give eternal life to those who believe. I believe that Jesus died for me, and I receive His love and forgiveness. I accept and am willing for the Lord to change me and bring me into the fullness of what He has planned for me. I want my life to glorify God and bring Him joy. I'm a simple girl with a simple life. I don't use elaborate words or try to impress anyone. I just want to live my life for Jesus. My life is my worship to the Lord.

Everyone has their own story and this one is mine. I felt compelled to share my life with you and be transparent in the hope of helping you through your own struggles and life experiences. I wanted to share how faithful our God in heaven is and how much love He has for all of us. I want to encourage you to never give up because there is always hope with God. It is my story, but some of it can be yours also. If you let Jesus into your heart, you will be amazed at the journey on which He will lead you. If you already have, then I encourage you to take the next step and let God have His way in your life. We are all unique, and each journey will never be the same, but what an adventure life is with God leading the way. Wherever you are, He is waiting patiently for you and eager to help you on your journey.

About the Author

Cynthia Ackerman and her husband of thirty-seven years live in Central New York. She is a mother of two grown children and grandmother of two girls. Cynthia has been a cosmetologist for forty years and has worked with high school students for the past fourteen years. Faith has been an essential influence through many trials in Cindy's life. Her family has been her biggest accomplishment and she takes great pride in the love that they share together.

Cynthia can be contacted on Facebook or at:
cynthiaackerman10@gmail.com

We are a Christian-based publishing company that was founded in 2009. Our primary focus has been to establish authors.

"5 Fold Media was the launching partner that I needed to bring *The Transformed Life* into reality. This team worked diligently and with integrity to help me bring my words and vision into manifestation through a book that I am proud of and continues to help people and churches around the world. None of this would have been possible without the partnership and education I received from 5 Fold Media."

- Pastor John Carter, Lead Pastor of Abundant Life Christian Center, Syracuse, NY, Author and Fox News Contributor

The Transformed Life is foreworded by Pastor A.R. Bernard, received endorsements from best-selling authors Phil Cooke, Rick Renner, and Tony Cooke, and has been featured on television shows such as TBN and local networks.

5 Fold Media
5701 E. Circle Dr. #338, Cicero, NY 13039
manuscript@5foldmedia.com

Find us on Facebook, Twitter, and YouTube.

Discover more at www.5FoldMedia.com.

CPSIA information can be obtained
at www.ICGtesting.com
Printed in the USA
BVHW03s0203060618
518339BV00019B/165/P